ITINERANT MINISTRY

Preparing to Go Into All the World

Jerry Crow

Red River Ministries

Copyright © 2024 Red River Ministries

Scripture quotations are from The ESV ® Bible (The Holy Bible, English Standard Version ®), copyright © 2001 by Crossway, a publishing ministry of Good News Publishers. Used by permission. All rights reserved.

All rights reserved. This book or any portion thereof may not be reproduced or used in any manner whatsoever without the express written permission of the publisher except for the use of brief quotations in a review.

Printed by Red River Ministries, in the United States of America.

ISBN: 9798874035556

First printing, 2024.

www.redriverministries.org

This book is dedicated to those who do not have a church that they consistently preach in, but rather have the privilege of taking the Word of God to a different group of people each week. It is my hope that this book helps you in your journey.

As always, this book is also dedicated to my loving wife, my closest friend, and my dearest companion, Cecelia. Without her support nothing in this ministry would get accomplished and I would fall apart. Thank you.

CONTENTS

Title Page

Copyright

Dedication

Foreword

Part 1 – Reconnaissance 1

Part 2 – Readiness 8

Part 3 – Release the Message 16

Part 4 – Reaching Out 20

Survey Responses 23

About The Author 25

FOREWORD

While it may seem strange to some people to see a guide book for itinerant ministers, I think it is necessary. This highly important task within the church is often overlooked. Education is focused on those who will become pastors or perhaps educators, but little attention is given to those who travel to bring forth the Word of God.

Some men are not giften with pastoral abilities. Some men are not afforded the opportunity to pastor a church. Still others simply are not called to the pastoral ministry, but they are still called to preach and proclaim the Word of God.

Sometimes itinerant ministers are called evangelists. Sometimes they are called traveling ministers. Sometimes a church may refer to them as a visiting preacher. Whatever name is given to them, there have been some great men in the past who were itinerant ministers.

One of the greatest itinerant ministers to ever preach the Word of God, at least in the last four hundred years, was George Whitefield. Whitefield was one of the main catalysts of the Great Awakening in the early 1700's. He was responsible for leading countless souls to Christ. May it be the same for those who read this book and use the practical advice within to help them in their ministry.

Yes, this is more of a practical guide than a spiritual guide. It is also not meant to teach you how to prepare sermons. I already have a book for that which you can also use to help in your ministry. (See my book *Introduction to Preaching: Preparing an Expository Sermon.*) This guide will help you along each step that you take, from contacting a church to what happens after you minister.

It is my prayer that those who read this book and use it will be better prepared in their ministry and will continue using this book throughout the rest of their ministry. Thank you and may God bless you all.

Introduction

Are you preparing to be an itinerant minister; or are you already engaged in ministering from church to church?

Do you have questions about where to begin, what to ask churches, or what you should be doing when you get asked to speak at a church?

This booklet is written with the hope of being able to answer these questions, and more. The four parts this book are here to help guide you through every step along the way, from starting a conversation with a new church to staying in contact with them after you leave.

This booklet is the result of years of being an itinerant preacher and being an associate pastor in a church. It is my desire to help those called to this important ministry to be the absolute best that they can possibly be.

This guide is not an all-inclusive how to prepare a sermon or anything like that. I have already authored a book to help with that. (See my book *Introduction to Preaching: Preparing an Expository Sermon.*) Instead, this guide will give steps to follow when contacting, and staying in contact with, a church.

So, for those who would like some advice on this all-important aspect of ministry, I invite you to turn the page and read on. This is a short read, but I am sure this little booklet will be packed with information you will use for years to come in your ministry.

PART 1 – RECONNAISSANCE

It is always a good idea to have some kind of idea what kind of church you might be asked to go to for ministry. This section will give you some ideas of what kind of questions you need to ask, both yourself and the contact person at the church. As we all know, the best way to get information is to ask questions, usually open-ended questions are most preferable. The more you can get your contact to talk, the more information you will gain.

One thing to note about this reconnaissance phase of the church contact process, you want to gain this information as early in the process as possible. Usually, it is best to get this information as soon as the church shows interest in bringing you in for a service. The day you set a date is the day you need to have this information made available to you.

Here are the questions with a brief explanation of the information you should gather from the answers to each one. Some of these questions may seem odd at first, but when you realize that not every church, even within a denomination, is the same these questions will begin to make more sense to you.

What denomination is the church affiliated with or closely related to?

This question might seem like an easy one to answer. After all, one need only look at the name of the church to see if there is a denominational affiliation listed. If there is not a denomination listed we can at least presume they are either independent or non-denominational, right?

While this might usually work, simply looking at the name of the church and seeing the name "Baptist" might not get any conclusive answer to this question. After all there are a multitude of distinct types of "Baptist" churches. Also, one of the major doctrines of "Baptist" churches is the autonomy of the local church.

This means that we may run across four different churches who are in the same association who have different major beliefs and the only thing that holds them together is the fact that they stick to credobaptism and a congregational style of church polity. One may hold to KJV only while another uses the ESV or NKJV. One may allow anyone to participate in communion while another may only allow church members to participate in communion. They may have different views on the appropriate age to baptize a new believer.

Some churches can give away a lot of information

about themselves by their name. Most of the time, any church that is associated with the Assemblies of God will have similar beliefs. Their worship styles may be different from one local church to the next, but when it comes time for the ministry of the Word and the operation of the gifts of the Holy Spirit, they will all believe the same.

The point is every church is different. That is why the next questions are also important.

What is the doctrine of the church?

To answer this question, you may not need to actually ask your contact person. If the church has a website, most churches have some kind of Statement of Faith posted. This can help to determine what the doctrine of the church may be. However, this may not always be the case. Some churches find a Statement of Faith that looks good to them, or that comes from a like-minded church, and they simply copy and paste the information.

Then again, the church may not have a website for you to check. This is where you ask your contact person for the information. Ask them to get specific about it, also. For example:

Is the church Arminian or Calvinist in their soteriology?

Is the church liturgical or more free in their worship style?

What is the church's official stance on certain social

issues?

The more information you can gain here, the easier it will be to prepare your sermon. Also, you may find that you are not a good fit for that particular church because you do not agree with them on some foundational doctrinal belief. If that is the case, be courteous to them and, if possible, recommend someone you know who holds to a similar doctrine.

What are the service times at the church?

This is rather basic information; however, it is one of the most important things you will need to know. The answer to this question tells you how many services the church has. Many churches have gone to multiple services on Sunday mornings. If you are not prepared for that possibility, it would not be a pleasant surprise.

What time does the church expect you to arrive?

Again, this seems like basic information. However, knowing if the church wants you to attend the Sunday School service would be good. Also, do they need you there early to get Scripture references from you for their technology department? (If that is the case, please give them all of your Scriptures and give them in the correct order.) Some churches like to meet with the visiting minister before the service starts just to go over the final details.

These are all valid reasons to be expected to arrive early. If the service begins at 10:00 am and the church asks you to arrive at 9:30 am, that is perfectly normal. This gives you time to pray, look over your notes, and mentally prepare yourself one last time.

How long does the service last?

Some churches are extremely strict about their time. If the service ends at 12:00, they want to be walking out the door at 12:00, not waiting for you to finish your last point at 12:05. Simply put, be courteous of the time. If you were a pastor and someone were visiting your church you would expect them to do the same.

What is the time limit for the preaching service?

This goes along with the last question, in a way. If the church is accustomed to a thirty-minute sermon time, you will lose them if you try to go forty-five minutes. Again, be courteous of the time. This will help to ensure that you get a return request as well. Many ministers are not as courteous of the time they are allotted and go well over their limits. Stick within the parameters you are given.

What is expected of you after you preach?

This is where things can get interesting. If you are a preacher who does not generally give a typical "altar call" but that is expected in the church you are visiting, they might expect you to do that. This is something that is good to be aware of before you make preparations to go to the church, and not the day you arrive. Some other things churches may expect of you are:

Greeting the congregation.

Praying for people.

Meeting with the board of the church.

Going to lunch with someone in the church.

There are many other valid things that a church may ask you to do after you have preached. If there is something you are uncomfortable with, let them know. Do not be afraid to speak up when you are uncomfortable about a situation. This will let them know why you may not be doing one of the things that most other ministers that come to the church does.

What version of the Bible does the church primarily use?

This is a huge question. The answer to this question will make your sermon preparation easier from the first moment you sit down. It will also help you to be relatable to the church.

If you primarily use the NASB but the church you are going to uses the ESV, it would be more than a good idea to use the same translation when you are preparing your sermon. This way the congregation can follow you easier. Also, the technology department does not have to search for a different version of the Bible in their computer program. If you use the same version their pastor uses a majority of the time, they will already have it pulled up in their program.

Will the church allow you to set up a book or merchandise table?

This one may not apply to everybody. However, if you have books or merchandise that you want to take with you to offer for sale at the church, this is a good thing to ask about at the beginning of the process. It will allow them to make sure they have a spot for you to set up. It will allow you to ensure you have enough inventory as well as a person to run said table. If they do not allow a book or merchandise table, now is a suitable time to know that as well.

PART 2 – READINESS

The information covered in this section will help you prepare to go to the church. You may want to do some of these during the reconnaissance phase, or you can wait until closer to time for you to go to the church. Either way, there are some delicate details that you will still need to work out with your contact person at the church.

The rest of the information covered in this section is what you will need to do personally. It will give you an opportunity to make any changes and revisions necessary to your plans. Whenever possible, this phase should be complete within a month of the date of you going to the church. There may be an exception or two and we will cover those in their own heading.

How are you going to travel to the church?

This question often gets overlooked in the process, especially for those of us who do our booking ourselves. Most of the time we do not consider our travel as part of the ministry, but it absolutely is crucial to how we will feel physically.

If we are travelling several states away and would rather drive than fly, then it may be a clever idea to arrive a day early for rest. If you are travelling to another country, this will give you opportunity to ensure you have all the necessary documentation needed to enter that country: passport, visa, etc.

It is also necessary to look at who will be paying for the travel expenses. None of us really like to think about this part of ministry, but it is something we must consider. Whoever is responsible for travel expenses will need to know in advance to ensure they are able to thoughtfully plan and make any reservations that may be necessary.

Are you going to need housing before or during the time you will be ministering at the church?

This question goes hand-in-hand with the previous question. If you are going to the next town over, or somewhere within a reasonable distance, this may not be an issue. However, if you are going somewhere that is some distance from where you live, or will be ministering for multiple days, this will need to be addressed.

Again, the same rule applies here for the payment. Whoever is responsible to pay for housing will need to know in advance to make reservations. Also, if you are staying at a hotel, you may want to consider the distance between the hotel and the church when you are planning the rest of your stay. While the hotel might be close to the airport, it could be some distance from the church.

Do not be afraid to stay with a couple from the church. This is most likely part of the hospitality team at the church, and it is part of their ministry. If it is the pastor, that is even better. It gives them an opportunity to practice part of the calling of a pastor.

1Timothy 3:1-5 *The saying is trustworthy: If anyone aspires to the office of overseer, he desires a noble task. Therefore, an overseer must be above reproach, the husband of one wife, sober-minded, self-controlled, respectable, <u>hospitable,</u> able to teach, not a drunkard, not violent but gentle, not quarrelsome, not a lover of money. <u>He must manage his own household well, with all dignity keeping his children submissive, for if someone does not know how to manage his own household, how will he care for God's church</u>?* (Emphasis added)

Prepare your sermon.

This should be a given. However, some people will just go to a file, pull out something they have preached so many times they have it almost memorized, and take it to preach.

Take time to prepare something new. Take time to get into the Word of God and take a fresh sermon to every church you visit. This will do two extremely important things in your life.

First, it will help you keep the Bible as the center of

your ministry. While you may be a dynamic speaker, your words do not matter unless they are Bible-centered. If you want to be a motivational speaker, that is fine. Do not do it in a church and do not do it under the guise of ministry. If what you have to say is not based around and pointing to what the Bible says, it does not belong in the church.

Second, it will keep you from being lazy when it comes to sermon preparation. As tempting as it is to have a circulation of about five, maybe ten, sermons that you just rotate in and out when you are traveling, this is honestly laziness. Prepare a new sermon for every service unless you are preaching at a church that has multiple services on a Sunday morning. Then, and only then, is it acceptable to repeat your sermon.

Remember that you are not the pastor of this church. With that in mind, it is not your responsibility to try to correct something that you think may be going wrong in the church. If you think the church is practicing some doctrinal error, it is not up to you to try to change the course of the church. You are not there to cause division. You are there to bring the Word of God to His people.

Also, when you prepare your sermon, make sure it is not man-centered, but it is God-centered. Too often in this day we have man-centered sermons, and this has made the church anemic, weak, and self-focused. Instead, we must have God-centered sermons to point people to the only One who can set them free from the bondage of sin. We must lose the idea that the church belongs to us and grab on to the fact that when we come together we are coming together to meet with, worship, and hear from God.

In his masterful work, *Preaching and Preachers,* Dr. Martyn Lloyd-Jones reminds his readers of this when he says the following:

"It is not our service; the people do not come there to see us or to please us. ... They, and we, are there to worship God, and to meet with God. ... A minister in a church is not like a man inviting people into his home; he's not in charge there. He's just a servant himself."

And also:

"I can forgive a man a bad sermon, I can forgive the preacher almost anything if he gives me a sense of God, if he gives me something for my soul. If he gives me the sense that he is inadequate in himself, that he is handling something which is very great and glorious. If he gives me some dim glimpse of the majesty and glory of God, the love of Christ my Savior, and the magnificence of the gospel. If he does that, I am his debtor, and I am profoundly grateful to him."

Prepare your heart, mind, and body.

The act of preaching is one of the most rigorous physical and mental activities you will ever participate in. It is also one of the most emotional activities ever known. If you have not properly prepared yourself for preaching, you can finish the act and be overwhelmed by emotion and tiredness, even to the point of exhaustion.

Dr. Martyn Lloyd-Jones said, "Preaching is the closest a man will ever come to the experience of childbirth."

This is where you must ensure that you are physically fit, emotionally strong, and mentally well prepared. You do not have to be a world-class athlete, fully prepared for a marathon or anything like that. However, some physical fitness is helpful. Stamina is important when you are preaching, especially if you are preaching over a period of multiple days with travel thrown in the mix. Some exercise and a good diet are crucial to your physical well-being.

Preaching is also an emotional act. You are dealing with the souls of men and women. You are delivering to them the Gospel of Jesus Christ and hoping that they respond positively. If you are unable to weep over the condition of lost souls or rejoice over the soul that comes to repentance, it may be time to reconsider your emotional priorities.

Preaching, when done properly, is a mentally taxing action. Let's face it, remembering everything that we have learned about a particular Scripture, even if we have notes in front of us, can be difficult. Then we have to decide how much to give to the people. If we give them all the information we have learned, we could be there for hours, and they probably would not be able to handle it. Paring down all the information we have about a particular subject or verse is a mental act that forces us to decide what is best for the listener.

Choose your wardrobe.

This may seem a little strange, at first. However, your clothing choice really matters. When you are behind the pulpit delivering the Word of God to the people of God, you are a messenger, an ambassador, of God. You want to dress appropriately for the role that you are undertaking.

If you are going to wear a suit, make sure it is clean and pressed and everything fits correctly. Take multiple shirts and ties with you, just in case one combination does not look right when you put it on. If you are not comfortable with the way you look, it will affect the way you feel the rest of the day.

At the same time, you do not want to wear something that will bring all the attention to you. Remember that you are God's ambassador, not a representative of you. You are there to point people to God, not to distract them with your shiny suit or over-polished shoes.

Do you have enough inventory for your book or merchandise table?

Again, this goes back to the answer to this question in the reconnaissance phase. If the church allows you to set up a table, make sure you have enough inventory to fill it and have a surplus backstock for high demand. Many times, people have underestimated the amount of inventory they might need.

A lack of inventory may lead to people being upset they are not able to purchase something they really wanted from you and you missing out on a sale. Also, ensure you have business cards with your contact information, social media, or your website, if you have one, available for people to be able to follow your ministry and be informed about new books or merchandise you may have available in the future.

PART 3 – RELEASE THE MESSAGE

This section will cover the day of the service. Whether you are preaching a Sunday morning, one time service, or a multi-day, multi-service event, this section will help you understand what you should do at that time.

Be punctual!

This cannot be stressed enough. When the church has an expectation of the time you should be there, make sure you are there at that time. It would be better to arrive before that time. It has been well said, "Early is on time, on time is late, and don't ever be late."

It is a good practice to arrive at least five to ten minutes before the church expects you. This will give you plenty of time for any last-minute additions or subtractions to your sermon before you give your Scripture references to the technology department of the church. It will give you time for a restroom break, if needed. It will give extra time to meet with people. It will also give you a little extra time to set up your book or merchandise table, if that has not already been done.

Respect the time limit you are given.

We have all been in services where a visiting minister will be going along preaching and look at the clock. He may say something like, "I only have five minutes, but I think you need to hear this." This is a highly disrespectful move. The church may be gracious at the moment and let the minister finish speaking, but they will remember that he is not respectful of their time.

When you are in the reconnaissance phase, one of the questions you should have asked was about the time limit you will have for the preaching of the Word. If the church does not give you a time limit, make sure you leave about ten minutes from the end of the message to the end of the service time.

Preach the Word.

Before we are able to preach the Word to the people, we must have first preached it to ourselves. This is the only way we can know that what we are about to say to the people is the truth of the Word of God and not our own man-made inventions.

Dr. Martyn Lloyd-Jones once said, "We have nothing to say to our people till first the Bible has been preached to ourselves."

1 Timothy 4:6-16 *If you put these things before the brothers, you will be a good servant of Christ Jesus,* *being trained in the words of the faith and of the good doctrine that you have followed. Have nothing to do with irreverent, silly myths. Rather train yourself for godliness; for while bodily training is of some value, godliness is of value in every way, as it holds promise for the present life and also for the life to come. The saying is trustworthy and deserving of full acceptance. For to this end, we toil and strive, because we have our hope set on the living God, who is the Savior of all people, especially of those who believe. Command and teach these things. Let no one despise you for your youth, but set the believers an example in speech, in conduct, in love, in faith, in purity. Until I come, devote yourself to the public reading of Scripture, to exhortation, to teaching. Do not neglect the gift you have, which was given you by prophecy when the council of elders laid their hands on you. Practice these things, immerse yourself in them, so that all may see your progress. Keep a close watch on yourself and on the teaching. Persist in this, for by so doing you will save both yourself and your hearers.*

It is the duty of every person who steps foot in the pulpit to preach the Word of God. We are not to preach our opinions, only to exhort and teach that which the Scripture says. If we go beyond that mandate and bring anything else into the pulpit, be it politics, current events, (except where Scripture touches those things which are happening today, and only if the Scripture we are preaching from happens to address anything happening currently in the world) or anything else that takes away from the teaching and exhortation of the Scripture, then it should be the duty of the leaders of the church we are speaking in to take us aside and correct us.

Respect the church's expectations.

Remember that one of the questions you should have asked during your reconnaissance phase was about the church's expectations after the preaching was completed. Be respectful of those requests, as long as it is something you are comfortable with doing. Your response to these requests and expectations will go a long way in determining whether the church asks you to come back another time to minister for them.

PART 4 – REACHING OUT

This section will cover what happens after the service has been completed and you have returned home. Following the advice given here will keep you in the minds of the church leaders when they are in need of a minister again. It will also help them be able to recommend you to other churches with whom they may be associated.

Express your gratitude.

In today's world it is really easy to forget that we are grateful for every opportunity we have to minister the Word of God. Expressing that gratitude to the church should be one of the first things we do when we return home. Here are some basic rules for doing this:

First, make it personal. Call out names of the church leaders, those who took extra care of you while you were in the church, or anyone you may remember from your time there. Also, remember the hospitality and technical teams; these groups are often overlooked by visiting ministers and a special "Thank you" is always welcome.

Second, make it tangible. In this digital age, it is so easy to sit at the computer, or grab a smartphone and write out an email. However, there is something extra special about receiving a hand-written letter or card from someone that makes people remember who sent them that letter or card.

Third, make it specific. Did the church put you up in a pleasant hotel? Did you stay at a person's home? Did they give you any gifts while you were there? Did they have a special lunch or take you to an excellent restaurant? Be specific about these things so the people in the church, especially the leaders, will know that you are paying close attention to what was going on while you were their guest.

Fourth, make it quick. Do not wait more than a few days after you return home to send out your letter or card. This will make sure the church receives it within a week or two of you visiting their congregation.

Stay in touch.

Make sure you keep an appropriate amount of contact with the church and church leaders after your "Thank you" letter or card. An appropriate amount would be once, maybe twice a year. More than that and you may come off a little pushy. Less than that and it is possible that they may forget you.

What kind of information should you give the church? Send them a newsletter-type update of your ministry, after all, their financial support when you spoke at their church did allow you to continue going out and ministering to others. This will keep them apprised to your ministry and make them feel part of what you are accomplishing as well as keep you on their minds whenever they may need the services of a guest minister again.

SURVEY RESPONSES

Months before I sat down to write this booklet, I sent out a survey to numerous pastors. I asked some basic questions about having guest ministers in to speak in their churches and I would like to share the most relevant responses with you here. Some of the questions were for parts of the booklet that have already been addressed and they will not be found here. However, here are those that I believe will be helpful for you.

> Q: Would you prefer a visiting minister to have a set fee to come to a church, or to simply receive an offering from the church?

Overwhelmingly, most churches would rather not see a set fee, or honorarium, from the visiting minister. Many times, the church has a set amount that they give, and they take up an offering for the minister. The majority of those who responded to this question said that the offering is usually more than the honorarium amount, sometimes double or even triple what the minister would have requested.

Q: Do you allow visiting ministers to set up a table to sell books, CDs, DVDs, and other merchandise pertaining to their ministry when they come to your church?

Again, most churches said they do allow ministers to set up a table. Since this is part of the minister's work, they do not see it as any hindrance to his work in the church when he comes to preach.

Q: What have past visiting ministers done that has been beneficial to you or to your church?

The majority of pastors surveyed said that itinerant ministers have helped to reinforce the unity of the church, have helped to spark a hunger for evangelism, or have helped move the church into a deeper hunger for the Word of God than what the pastor was able to accomplish on his own.

ABOUT THE AUTHOR

Jerry Crow

I was raised in Southeast Oklahoma. Born to a young mother, my early childhood memories are filled with scenes of my grandmother, my mother and her brothers, and myself attending church as often as the doors were open. I can still remember the smell of the hymnals and the sound of the elder church members singing. I spent those early summers going to Vacation Bible School and later, when I was of sufficient age, Summer Church Camps.

As the years progressed I noticed a tugging in my spirit. I was not sure what this feeling meant and no one I asked could offer any guidance. This tugging began when I was nine years old. I knew what it meant to be saved, at least as much as I could. It was not until years later that I learned this tugging was a call to the ministry.

At the young age of seventeen I finally accepted salvation. I had gone through many trials in my young life, including a bout of depression which had me contemplating the end of my life. When I was saved it was a transformation that could only be described as a complete and total change of my spirit. Truthfully, I could only tell a difference in my spirit because my soul was still perplexed. I still struggled with depression and anxiety.

A few months after my conversion, I was baptized. It was an experience I will never forget. It was mid-March and we had a youth group camp at the lake. I should tell you that this lake is never warmer than seventy degrees even in the midst of one hundred plus degree weather and even less warm coming off a cold winter. I was one of five people being baptized that day. It was truly memorable and so was the campfire we all ran to afterward.

It was a couple more months and my pastor asked me if I would be willing to help with the youth group on Wednesday nights. After some prayer, I told him I would be delighted to help in any way I could. Our youth pastor had a job that kept him out every other week and it was up to me to fill in when he could not be there. This was my first real experience at teaching from the Bible. From that first Wednesday night I was hooked. I knew I had found my right place.

Due to some personal issues, I found myself a few years later in a completely foreign land. I had just moved from my home in the depths of Oklahoma to a seemingly hostile area known as Southern Illinois. It was not hostile at all as I was greeted warmly and welcomed into a congregation there with excitement.

My time in Illinois was spent evangelizing, singing, and as an associate pastor. I was ordained to ministry in 2007. Our church had a Bible college which met on Monday nights and I was invited to help with some of the classes there. It was as though I had found the most perfect position to ever exist. I was preaching regularly. I was teaching weekly, sometimes two classes. I was on the worship team. I was part of the pastoral team. I had found my place in the world and I could not have been happier.

It is a great joy and honor to me to be able to minister the Word of God to people. Whether it is a one-on-one basis, a class full of students, or a congregation filled with hungry listeners, it is my greatest pleasure to be able to break open the Bible and fill the ears and minds of the listeners with the truths of God's Word.

I am now in Oklahoma, again, with my wife and son who are absolutely wonderful. I love them both with all of my heart. They are supportive of my ministry and I could never thank them enough for that. Their support and love are part of what drives me every day. I am grateful to God that He put them in my life.

Made in the USA
Columbia, SC
01 April 2025